HANDWR

for Christian Schools®

COORDINATING WRITERS
Joyce Garland
Charlene Killian
Karen L. Wolf

Worktext Highlights

Theme:	Sights of America
Letter Presentation:	Similarities of Formation
Skills Emphasized:	Good Handwriting Posture Letter Formation Slant Consistency Alignment Spacing Neatness
Evaluation:	Pretest Periodic Assessments Posttest

As you use this book, you will learn more about America, our beautiful land blessed by God. The Sightseer family have their suitcases packed and are ready to go. Come on along!

Cover Photo Credits
Digital Stock: United States Flag, Washington Monument, Grand Tetons

HANDWRITING 4 for Christian Schools® Second Edition has been produced in cooperation with the Bob Jones Elementary School.
© 1984, 1996, 1999 by Bob Jones University Press.
Layout and design: Dick Mitchell and Patricia Tirado
Cover design: Holly Gilbert
Project editor: Lance Weldy
All rights reserved
ISBN-1-57924-263-4
Printing in the United States of America
15 14 13 12 11 10 9 8 7 6 5 4 3 2 1

Tour Guide Schedule

"America, the Beautiful"	4
Pacific States	8
Rocky Mountain States	19
Southwestern States	34
Middle West States	44
State Flags	66
Southern States	76
Northeast States	102

Consultants

Grace C. Hargis, Ph.D.
Walter G. Fremont, Ed.D.
Melva M. Heintz, M.A.
Janice A. Joss, M.A.T.
Philip D. Smith, Ed.D.
Hazel M. Truman, M.A.

America, the Beautiful

America, the Beautiful

O beautiful for spacious skies,
For amber waves of grain,
For purple mountain majesties
Above the fruited plain!
America! America!
God shed His grace on thee,
And crown thy good
    with brotherhood
From sea to shining sea.

       Katherine Lee Bates

Pretest

name ____________________

Write the words of the hymn "America, the Beautiful."

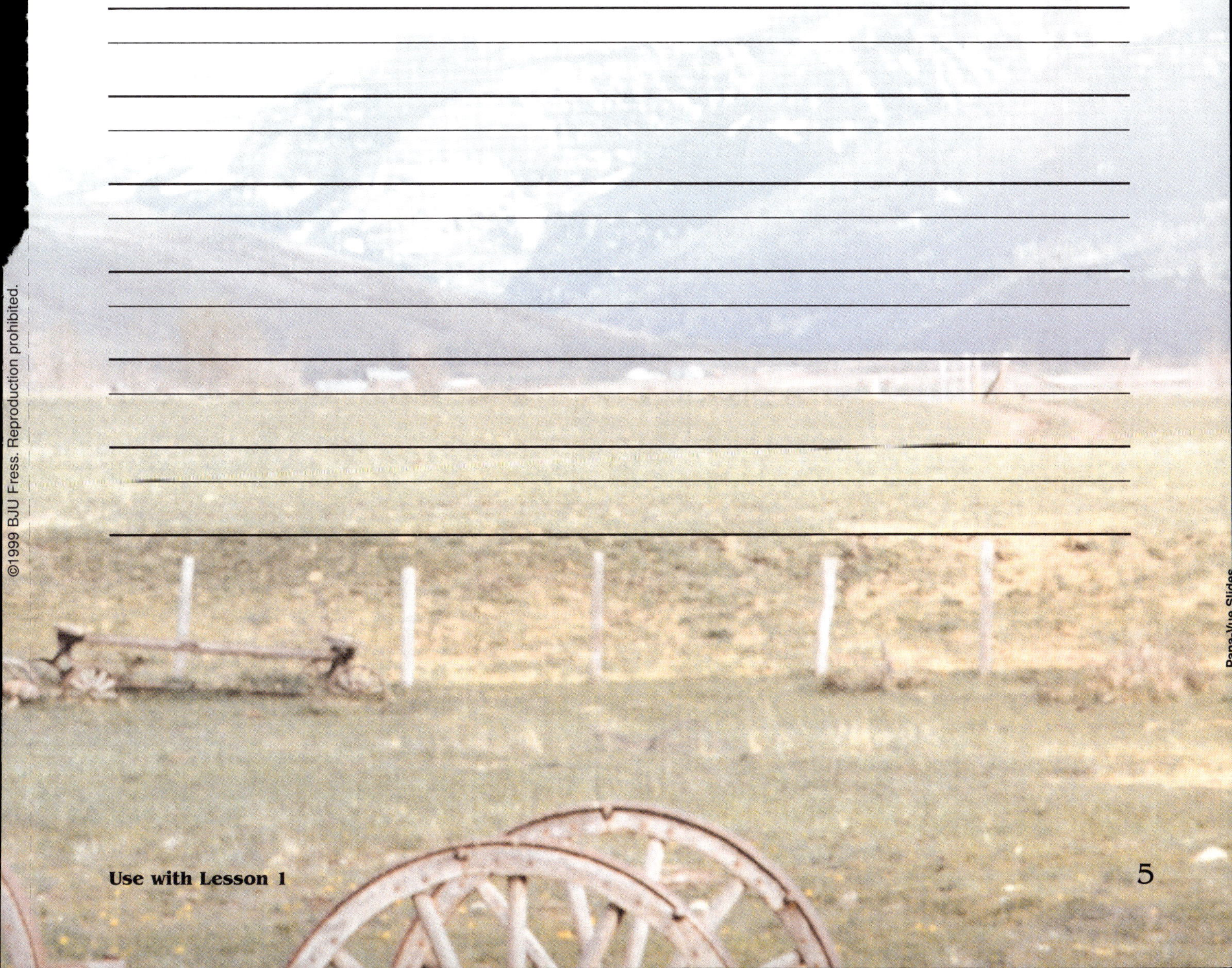

Pana-Vue Slides

America's Time Line

name _____

1 2 3 4 5 6 7 8 9 0

Write the correct dates on the lines. Use the numbers as an example.

2000

1950
★ **1961—** First American in space

★ **1939-1945—** World War II

1900
★ **1914-1918—** World War I

1850
★ **1861-1865—** Civil War

★ **1848-1849—** Gold Rush

1800
★ **1803—** Louisiana Purchase

★ **1788—** Constitution accepted

★ **1776—** Declaration of Independence

1750

1700

The first American traveled into space _____

in _____.

The Declaration of Independence was signed _____

in _____.

The thirteen colonies signed the Constitution _____

in _____.

The U.S. bought the Louisiana Purchase in _____

_____.

The Civil War split the U.S. from _____ _____

_____ to _____.

The Gold Rush attracted thousands in _____ _____

_____ and _____.

Use with Lesson 1

Mapping Out Good Handwriting

name _____

Hold the pencil about an inch from the point.

Bend forward slightly.

Rest your forearms on the desk.

Sit comfortably.

Place your feet on the floor.

Follow the instructions and answer the questions.

1. If you are bending slightly forward and not leaning to one side, write your name.
   _____
   _____

2. If both feet are on the floor, write today's date.
   _____
   _____

3. If your page is slanted correctly, write the name of your town.
   _____
   _____

4. If you are holding your pencil lightly about an inch from the point, write the name of your state.
   _____
   _____

Use with Lesson 2

name _____

PACIFIC STATES

~~Glue the flags in the correct places.~~ Write the names of the states in the blanks.

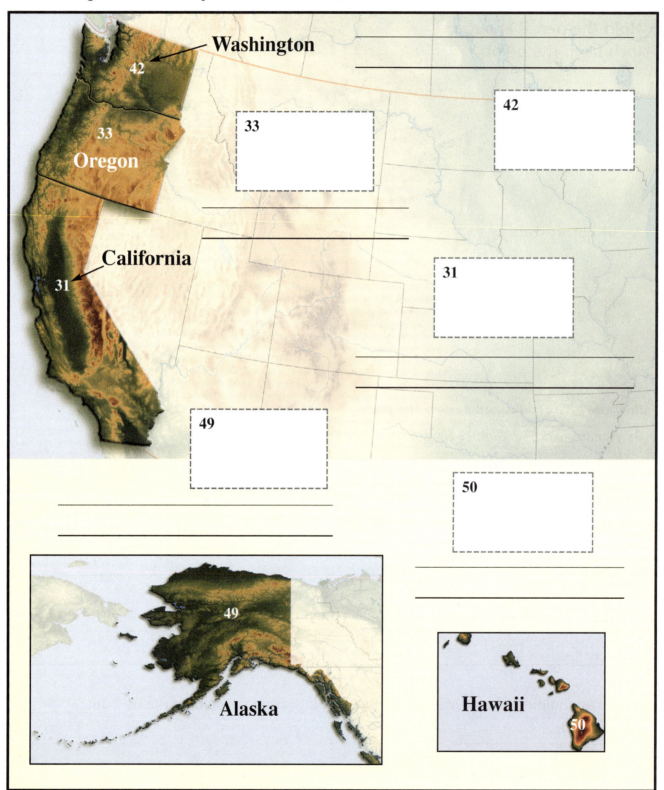

8   Use with Lesson 3

California's Land

name _____

Choose one of these photographs and write a description on handwriting paper.

Cc Aa Oo

California is the third largest state. Many cities spread for miles, but mountains, valleys, forests, and deserts cover much of the land. Huge tracts of this land have been preserved in national parks.

Yosemite National Park

Death Valley

"In his hand are the deep places of the earth: the strength of the hills is his also."
Psalm 95:4

Use with Lesson 4

California Gold Rush

name _____

In the 1800s prospectors flocked to California to pan for gold. In those years California earned its nickname: the Golden State.

Write each sentence under the correct picture.

Last I trade the gold for money.
First I stake out a claim.
Next I sift gold from junk rock.
Then I weigh the gold to find its value.

Use with Lesson 5

The Oregon Trail

name _____

Ll Jj

Hundreds of pioneers stocked their wagons with provisions and set out on the Oregon Trail in 1843. For six months they battled floods, Indians, and sickness across two thousand miles to the Pacific Ocean. There they built homes, planted fields, and tamed the wilderness of America.

Write the following poem on handwriting paper.

> The Oregon Trail
> Two hundred wagons,
>   Rolling out to Oregon,
> Breaking through the gopher holes,
>   Lurching wide and free,
> Crawling up the mountain pass,
>   Jolting, grumbling, rumbling on,
> Two hundred wagons,
>   Rolling to the sea.
>   —Arthur Guiterman

THE OREGON TRAIL: 1843 by Arthur Guiterman from I SING THE PIONEER, 1954. Reprinted by permission of Louise H. Sciove.

OREGON TRAIL MUSEUM

Use with Lesson 6

Christian Pioneer

name _____

Ss Dd

Jedediah Strong Smith trapped, traded, and explored for his living. The first white man to cross the wilderness of Oregon, Smith is remembered as a rugged pioneer, but other trappers called him the "American Paul." He constantly witnessed for Christ to these ruthless men.

Smith always kept his saddlebag near him. It contained everything he needed for life in the wilderness. He knew he would be lost without it.

Smith kept these items for his life in the wilderness.

1. Bible
2. Hymnbook
3. Matthew Henry's Commentary
4. Traps and trap sack
5. Rifle
6. Knife
7. Bullet pouch
8. Whetstone
9. Pistols
10. Gunpowder

Write the items.

1. _____
2. _____
3. _____
4. _____
5. _____
6. _____
7. _____
8. _____
9. _____
10. _____

Use with Lesson 7

King of Fish

name _____

It Ff

Salmon from the creeks and riverbeds of Washington State journey to the sea. There they eat and grow. Finally, before dying, they return hundreds of miles to the same stream from which they were hatched. Swimming against rushing currents and jumping rocky barriers ten feet or higher, they travel on, not even stopping to eat. They search for a shallow gravel bed and at last lay their eggs. Their journey is over.

"And God said, Let the waters bring forth abundantly the moving creature that hath life."

Genesis 1:20a

Write the names of the kinds of salmon on the lines.

Pink Salmon

Chinook or Quinnat

Sockeye Salmon

Coho Salmon

Dog Salmon

Use with Lesson 8

13

Mount St. Helens

name _____

On May 18, 1980, Mount St. Helens in Washington State proved that she was more than just a mountain when she erupted with a mighty volcanic blast.

Cone—the part of the volcano above the ground

Sedimentary Rock— rock layers of crushed mud

Igneous Rock— cooled lava

Basalt—hard volcanic rock

Magma—hot, melted rock deep underground

Write the definition beside the words.

Basalt _____

Cone _____

Igneous Rock _____

Magma _____

Sedimentary Rock _____

14

Use with Lesson 9

Alaskan Eskimo

name _____

Mm Nn

The Eskimos of Alaska have learned to live in the cold, frozen northern land.

- Eskimos travel by dogsled.
- Sometimes Eskimos hunt polar bears.
- Thick fur clothes keep them warm.
- They cut holes in the ice to fish.
- They carve pictures on walrus tusks.
- They build skin-covered boats called oomiaks.
- Some Eskimos live in igloos.
- They hunt whales with long, sharp harpoons.

Write a paragraph about Eskimo people. Use the information on the igloo.

_____
_____
_____
_____
_____
_____
_____
_____
_____
_____
_____
_____

The Northern Lights

Pp Rr

In March and April, and in September and October, the northern lights often appear in the Alaskan skies. As darkness falls, the sky begins to glow in a bright yellow-green color. This glow in the sky is called the Aurora Borealis.

"For God, who commanded the light to shine out of darkness, hath shined in our hearts, to give the light of the knowledge of the glory of God in the face of Jesus Christ."

II Corinthians 4:6

Write the paragraph.

The Aloha State

name _____

Write the facts in chronological order on the lines below.

- Hawaii became the fiftieth state in 1959.
- The islands were first united in 1795 under King Kamehameha I.
- The first Christian missionaries arrived in 1820.
- Captain Cook discovered the islands in 1778.
- The Japanese attacked Pearl Harbor in 1941.

Pearl Harb. Digital Stock

PhotoDisc, Inc. (Top, right, bottom)

Use with Lesson 12

Hawaiian Animals

name _____

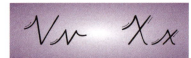

Write the names of the animals.

Hawaiian 'Iiwi

Nene

Surgeonfish

Moorish Idol

Humpback Whale

Monk Seal

name _____

ROCKY MOUNTAIN STATES

Glue the flags in the correct places. Write the names of the states in the blanks.

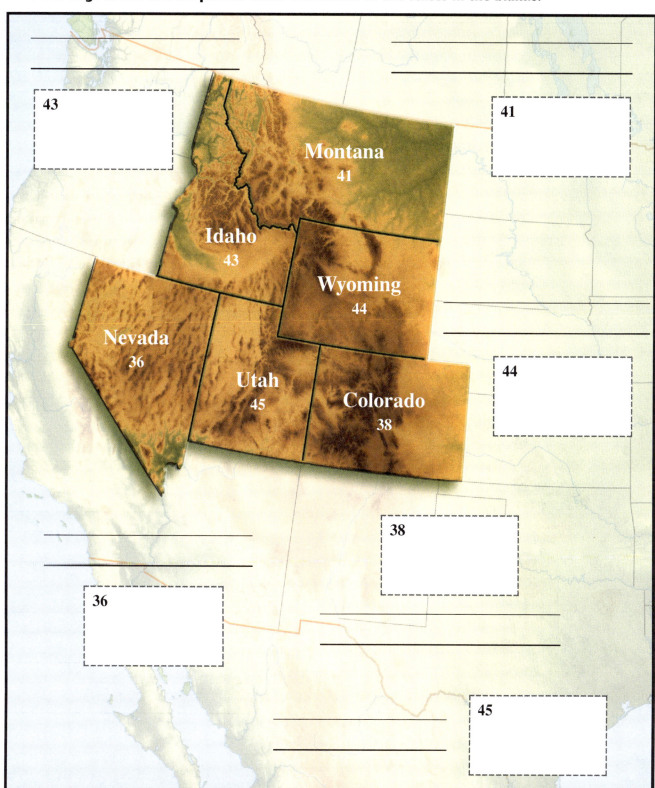

Use with Lesson 14

19

Handwriting Signs

name _____

Practice the punctuation. Write a sentence using the given punctuation.

Why?

Yes.

"Hi!"

I'm

235-5241

Use with Lesson 15

Idaho Potatoes

name ____________________

More potatoes grow in Idaho than in any other state.

Ww Yy Zz

Write the words in the blanks.

Potato Plant

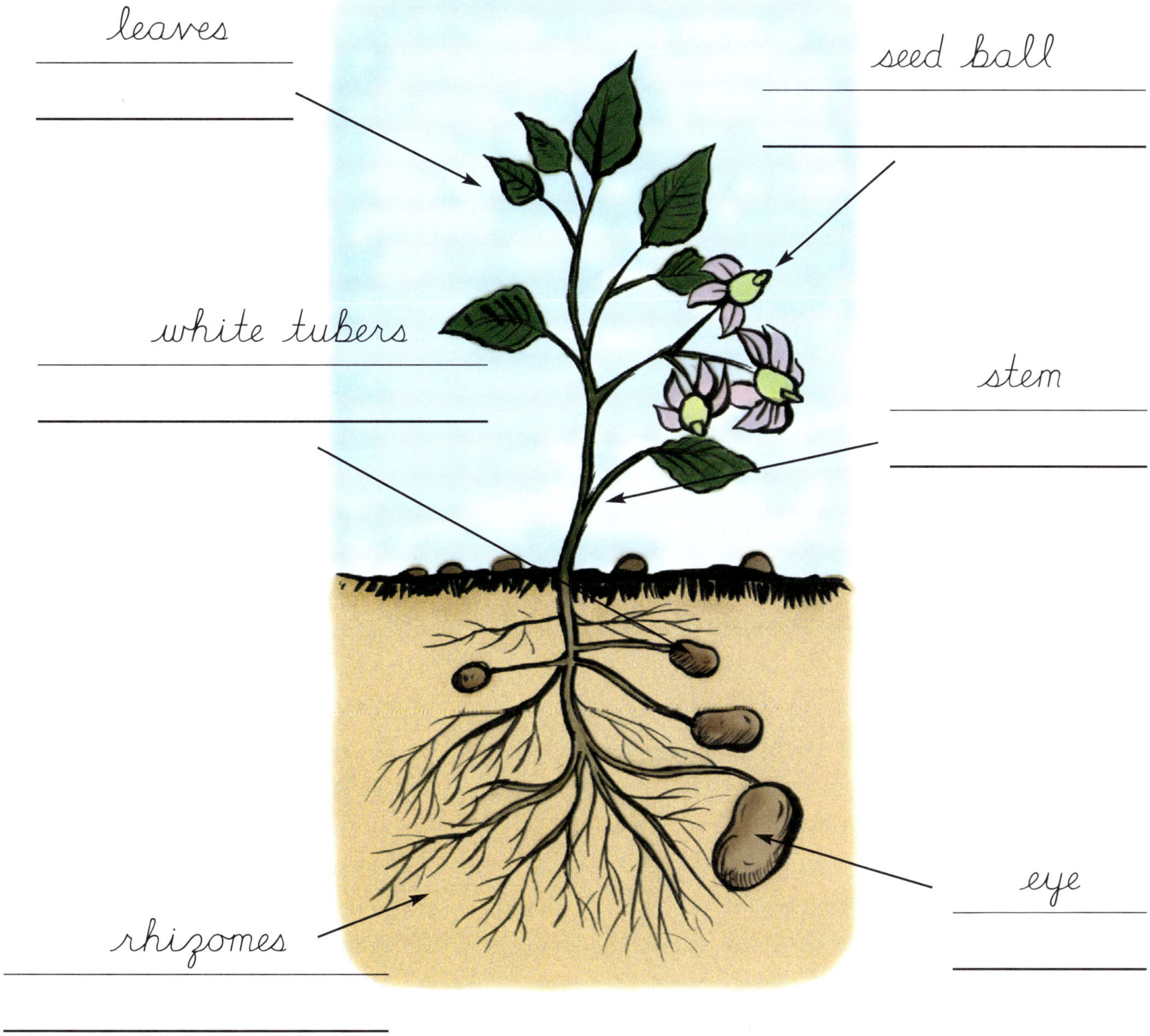
leaves
seed ball
white tubers
stem
eye
rhizomes

Idaho's Author

Vv Xx Uu

Write the report on notebook paper.

(Date) (Name)
(subject) (class)

Caddie Woodlawn
by Carol Ryrie Brink

Carol Ryrie Brink lived with her grandmother in Idaho. Her grandmother told her stories about pioneer days and Indian attacks. These were true stories that had happened to Carol's grandmother.

When Carol grew up, she wrote a book of these stories called Caddie Woodlawn. Carol Ryrie Brink won a Newbery Medal because her book is a great contribution to children's literature in America.

The Silver State

name _____

Write the paragraph below on handwriting paper.

Nevada's most common name is the Silver State. A vast amount of silver was taken from its mines. Mining towns attract thousands of tourists each year. Mining is still one of Nevada's main industries.

Sharpen Your Skills! **Write the letters.**

Aa

Use with Lesson 18

Skiing in Nevada

name _____

The mountains of Nevada glisten with snow for up to six months every year. Skiers can't resist the icy slopes. One by one they swoosh down the mountains, leaving two thin tracks behind them.

Write the names of the pieces of the skier's outfit.

- ski cap
- skis
- goggles
- poles
- gloves
- boots

Sharpen Your Skills!

Write the letters.

Bb

Use with Lesson 19

Great Salt Lake

name _____

The Great Salt Lake of Utah is the largest inland lake in America. Because no rivers flow out of it, its water is saltier than the ocean.

Area: 940 square miles

Elevation: 4,195 feet above sea level

Write the answers on the blanks.

1. List two cities located on the shore of the Great Salt Lake.
_____
_____

2. Name the rivers that flow into the Great Salt Lake.
_____
_____
_____

3. What is this symbol?
_____
_____

4. How many feet above sea level is the lake?
_____
_____

5. What is this symbol?
_____
_____

 Write the letters.

Use with Lesson 20

25

The Bible and Mormonism

name _____

Many Mormons live in Utah. They faithfully attend services held in their beautiful temples, but their trust is placed in man and his writings, rather than in the one true God.

Mormons teach:	**The Bible teaches:**
1. God was once a man.	1. God was always God.—*Psalm 90:2*
2. Man can become a god.	2. There will never be any other God.—*Isaiah 43:10*
3. There are many gods.	3. God is the one true God.—*Isaiah 44:6*

Choose one of the verses from the list that tells about God. Find the verse in your Bible and write it on the lines.

_____
_____
_____
_____
_____
_____
_____
_____
_____
_____
_____

Digital Stock

Write the letters.

Dd

Use with Lesson 21

Colorado Forest Fire

name _____

To protect Colorado's forests, fire towers dot the land and rangers keep a careful watch.

Firefighting Methods

1. Spray water on the flames.
2. Dig a fire line.
3. Shovel or bulldoze dirt on the fire.
4. Parachute smoke jumpers near the fire.
5. Drop chemicals from planes on the fire.

Write the methods for fighting forest fires.

Sharpen Your Skills! **Write the letters.**

E e

Use with Lesson 22

Roof of North America

name _____

The Rocky Mountains reach for the sky like a city of giant rooftops. Range after range crisscrosses Colorado's land.

Never Summers

Mosquitos

Rockies

Write the names of the mountain ranges in alphabetical order.

_____
_____
_____
_____
_____
_____
_____
_____
_____

Needles

Tarryalls

"Thy righteousness is like the great mountains . . .

. . . thy judgments are a great deep: O Lord, thou preservest man and beast."
Psalm 36:6

Grenediers

San Miguels

Elk

28

Use with Lesson 23

Wyoming's Old Faithful

name _____

Write the paragraph on handwriting paper.

"Remember his marvellous works that he hath done."
Psalm 105:5a

The geyser, Old Faithful, erupts every 65 minutes. It shoots 10,000 gallons of boiling water 170 feet into the sky. The minerals in the water create yellow, red, and green designs among the rocks. But Old Faithful is just one of the many natural wonders of Yellowstone Park in Wyoming.

Sharpen Your Skills!

Write the letters.

Ff

Use with Lesson 24

Dogies of Wyoming

name _____

Cowboys can be heard singing to their herds across the grass lands of Wyoming. The motherless calves, called dogies, listen contentedly as they feed on the rich green grass.

Write the words of the song on handwriting paper.

Get Along Little Dogies

As I was a-walkin' one mornin' for pleasure,
I spied a cowpuncher come ridin' along;
His hat was throwed back
   And his spurs was a-jinglin',
And as he approached he was singin' this
   song.

Whoopee ti yi yo, git along little dogies,
It's your misfortune and none of my own.
Whoopee ti yi yo, git along little dogies,
You know that Wyoming
   Will be your new home.

SHARPEN YOUR SKILLS! **Write the letters.**

Gg

Use with Lesson 25

Charles M. Russell, Montana's Artist

Sixteen-year-old Charles Russell traveled to Montana to become a cowboy. He loved the West, and before long he captured it on canvas. His friends nicknamed him the "Cowboy Artist." His paintings make the wild West come alive.

Courtesy of the Montana Historical Society, Gift of Col. Wallis Huidekoper

The Herd Quitter

Write these titles of Charles M. Russell's works of art.

Bronco Buster
Buffalo Hunting
The Horse Thieves
Indians Attacking
Grizzly
The Posse
Breaking Camp
Rattle Snake

Write the letters.

Hh

Montana's National Bison Range

Buffalo once roamed the plains by the thousands. Today very few are left. Montana established a National Bison Range to keep the buffalo alive.

1,600-2,800 lbs.

5½-6 feet

9-12 feet

American Buffalo or Bison

Height: _____

Length: _____

Weight: _____

Life span: _____

"For every beast of the forest is mine, and the cattle upon a thousand hills."
Psalm 50:10

Fill in the chart, and then use the information to write a description of the buffalo.

_____
_____
_____
_____
_____
_____
_____
_____
_____
_____

Sharpen Your Skills!

Write the letters.

Ii

Use with Lesson 27

Spacing

name _____

	Wrong		Right
Space within letters:	*e*	*e*	*e*
Space between letters:	*if*	*if*	
Space between words:	*he is*	*he is*	
Space between lines:	*Go*	*Go*	
	The	*The*	

Write your address on the line below. Be sure to space correctly.

_____
_____
_____
_____
_____
_____

Use with Lesson 28

name _____

SOUTHWESTERN STATES

Glue the flags in the correct places. Write the names of the states in the blanks.

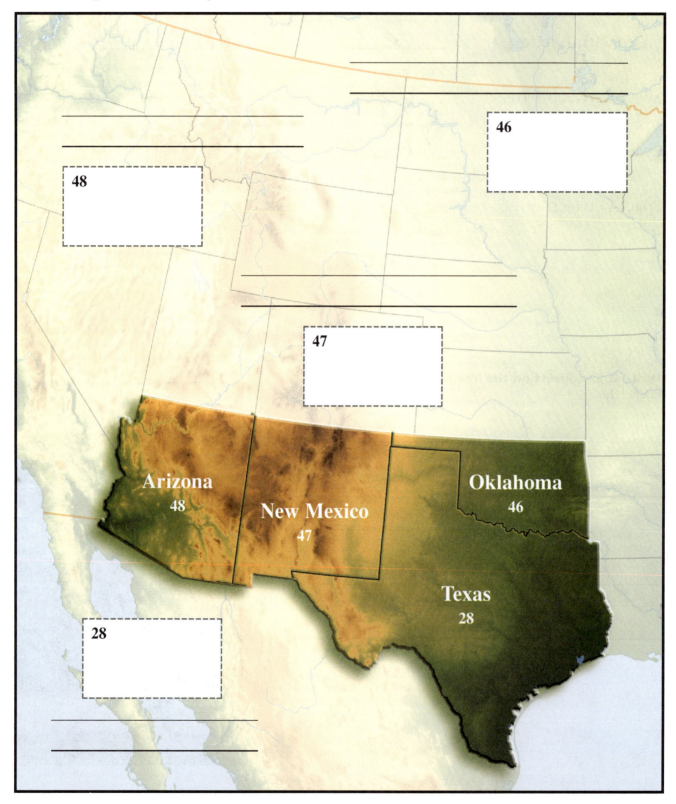

34 Use with Lesson 29

Arizona Pueblos

name _____

The peaceful Pueblo Indians built their mud homes, also called pueblos, high on cliffs for safety. A few Indians still live as their ancestors did, but most of the pueblos are unused.

Write the poem on handwriting paper.

Silent Pueblos

Silent and empty hang the houses on the cliff,
Proud and noble pueblos, standing straight and stiff.
No more spinning pottery wheel.
No more shuttle weaving.
No more pounding cornmeal.
No more people leaving.
All is silent on the cliffs and dark and still as night.
And the pueblos, proud but empty, fade beneath the light.

Sharpen Your Skills! **Write the letters.**

Jj

Use with Lesson 30

The Grand Canyon

name _____

Draw an X through the paragraph that is not true.

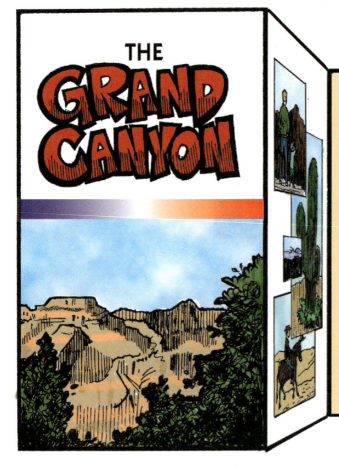

The Grand Canyon of Arizona is a colossal wonder 277 miles long and a mile deep.

Millions of years ago the Colorado River caused the land to erode. Today the exposed walls show the story of evolution in fossils.

You won't want to miss the cable-car ride across the canyon or the burro ride to the edge of the Colorado River on the canyon floor.

After the Flood, the Grand Canyon was soft, muddy land. Water rushed to the oceans, and mud was carried away to form the canyon. Slowly the muddy land hardened into rock. Sea fossils found in the canyon walls show that once the ocean covered the land. They also show that evolution is false.

Write the paragraph on handwriting paper that tells how the Flood caused the Grand Canyon.

Sharpen Your Skills!

Write the letters.

K k

The Santa Fe Trail

name _____

Read the paragraph.

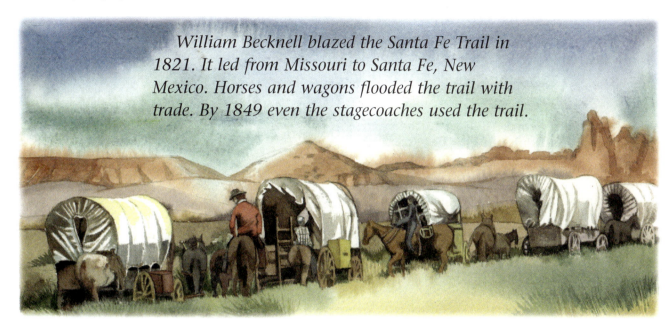

William Becknell blazed the Santa Fe Trail in 1821. It led from Missouri to Santa Fe, New Mexico. Horses and wagons flooded the trail with trade. By 1849 even the stagecoaches used the trail.

On the lines below write eight or more common and proper nouns from the paragraph above.

_____ _____
_____ _____
_____ _____
_____ _____
_____ _____
_____ _____
_____ _____
_____ _____

SHARPEN YOUR SKILLS!

Write the letters.

_Ll_ _____

Spanish New Mexico

name _____

Many Spanish people settled in New Mexico. Their towns and villages have Spanish names, and Spanish is spoken there often.

Write the Spanish word. Then write the English word you think it might be.

Hola
Americano
clase
carro

Nuevo Mexico
Los Estados Unidos

Sharpen Your Skills!

Write the letters.

Mm

38   Use with Lesson 33

Oklahoma's Cattle

name _____

> The ranchers in Oklahoma graze their cattle on the fertile rolling hills. Over four million cattle are raised there.

Write the words of the gospel song on handwriting paper.

He Owns the Cattle
John W. Peterson

He owns the cattle on a thousand hills,
The wealth in every mine;
He owns the rivers and the rocks and rills,
The sun and stars that shine;
Wonderful riches more than tongue can tell,
He is my Father, so they're mine as well;
He owns the cattle on a thousand hills,
I know that He will care for me.

HE OWNS THE CATTLE ON A THOUSAND HILLS (Peterson) © Copyright 1948 renewed 1976 by John W. Peterson Music Co. All rights reserved. Used by permission.

Use with Lesson 34

Rodeo

name _____

Write the rules under the correct events.

The rodeo is Oklahoma's favorite sport.

Hang on for ten seconds.
Tie up three legs of the calf.
Grab the steer by the horns.
Hold on with only one hand.
Lasso the calf to stop it.
Wrestle the steer to the ground.

Calf roping
_____
_____
_____

Steer dogging
_____
_____
_____

Bucking Bronco Ride
_____
_____
_____

Sharpen Your Skills!

Write the letters.

Nn _____

Use with Lesson 35

A Texan's Ministry

name _____

Roloff Evangelistic

In Texas the Lord gave Lester Roloff a burden to help hopeless boys and girls lost in sin. He cared for them in homes he built. His work continues to honor the Lord.

Write these verses on handwriting paper.

"For I was an hungred, and ye gave me meat: I was thirsty, and ye gave me drink: I was a stranger, and ye took me in."
"Inasmuch as ye have done it unto one of the least of these my brethren, ye have done it unto me."

Matthew 25:35; 40b

Sharpen Your Skills! **Write the letters.**

Oo

Use with Lesson 36

Cowboy Hats

name _____

Write the name of each hat.

A cowboy's hat could fan the sparks of the weakest campfire, haul water for miles, or even be used to pillow the cowboy's weary head. Without his hat a cowboy didn't feel properly dressed.

Lone Star

Old Fort Worth

Brushpopper

Boss of the Plains

Longhorn

King Ranch Camp

Vaquero

Sharpen Your Skills! **Write the letters.**

Pp

Slant Check

name _____

**Draw diagonal lines to check the slant of each word.
Draw an *X* beside the incorrectly slanted words.**

town	city X	state
country	place	land
world	country	people
friend	family	home

**Write the name of your church. Draw diagonal
lines to check the slant.**

_____

_____

_____

name _____

MIDDLE WEST STATES

Glue the flags in the correct places. Write the names of the states in the blanks.

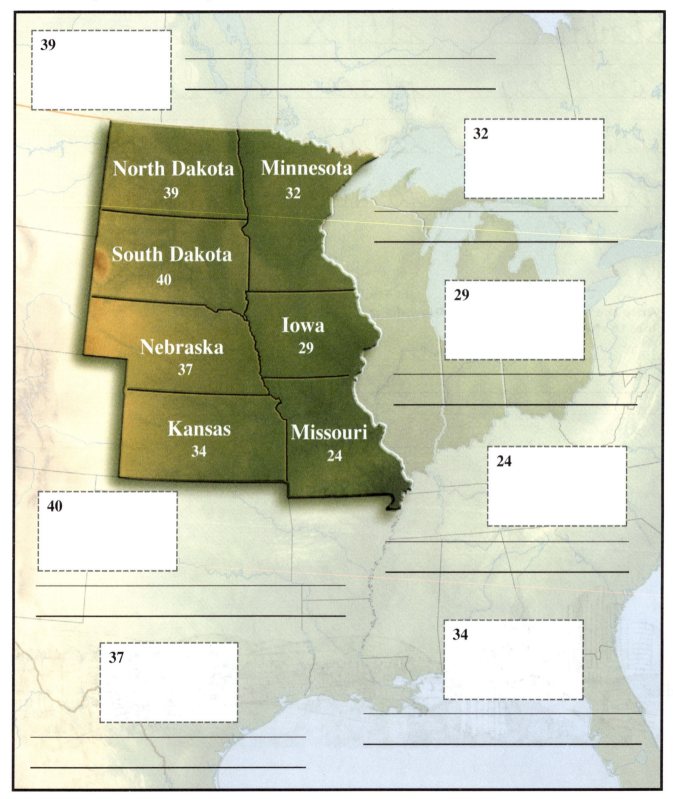

44 Use with Lesson 39

name _____

MIDDLE WEST STATES (CONT'D)

Glue the flags in the correct places. Write the names of the states in the blanks.

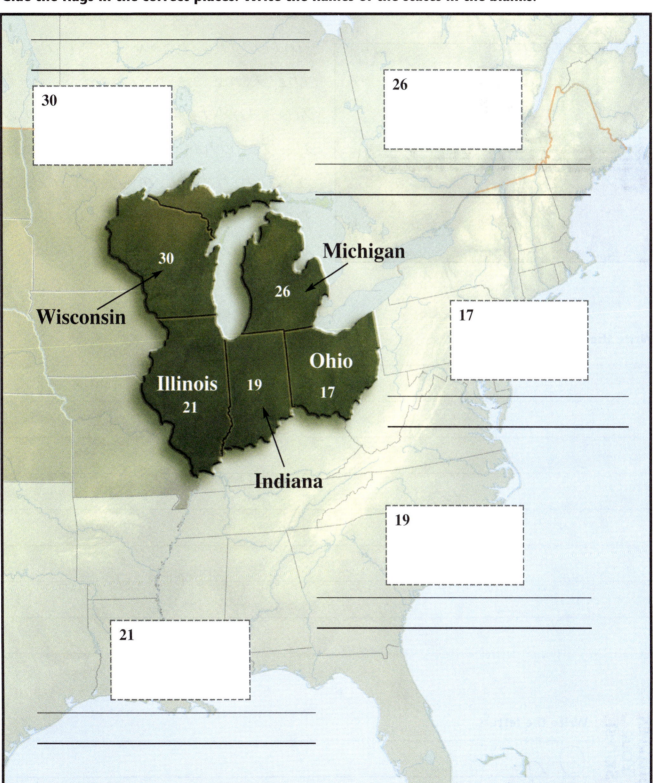

Use with Lesson 39

45

North Dakota Farming

name _____

The rolling hills of North Dakota produce a golden harvest of wheat each year.

Let both grow together until the harvest: and in the time of harvest I will say to the reapers, Gather ye together first the tares, and bind them in bundles to burn them: but gather the wheat into my barn.
Matthew 13:30

Write the verse below.

SHARPEN YOUR SKILLS!

Write the letters.

Qq

Use with Lesson 40

The Badlands

name _____

The name badlands *describes the bare, rocky land in western North Dakota, but not everything about the badlands is bad.*

Coal, clay, and limestone are mined there.
Nothing grows well.
Many of the hills and ravines are beautiful.
Travel was slow and difficult.
Indians and bandits hid in the hills.

Write each sentence under the appropriate heading– Good Things or Bad Things.

Good Things

_____
_____
_____
_____

Bad Things

_____
_____
_____
_____

Write the letters.

Rr _____

Use with Lesson 41

Mount Rushmore

name _____

Mount Rushmore is located in the Black Hills of South Dakota. On this granite cliff is a huge carving that shows the faces of four great American presidents.

Write the sentences.

The Mount Rushmore National Memorial shows the faces of George Washington, Thomas Jefferson, Theodore Roosevelt, and Abraham Lincoln. It is over 500 feet high.

Sharpen Your Skills! **Write the letters.**

Ss

Use with Lesson 42

South Dakota

name _____

Draw lines to match the facts and the illustrations. Write the facts on handwriting paper in chronological order.

The great Sioux leader Sitting Bull was killed near Little Eagle in 1890.

Gold was discovered, and Deadwood became a booming mining town in 1876.

In 1831 the steamboat *Yellowstone* proved that the upper Missouri could be traveled.

The minuteman missiles were completely installed and usable by 1963.

Line Change

name _____

Practice writing the verse. Follow the example.

Do not let ascenders run into descenders.
Do not let uppercase letters run into descenders.

If ye be willing and obedient, ye shall eat the good of the land.
— Isaiah 1:19

Use with Lesson 44

On The Line

Keep tall letters the same height.
Keep short letters the same height.
Use the lines as guides.

Finish the sentence with several answers. Watch the lines.

I love America because

Settling Nebraska

name _____

The settlers of Nebraska, called Sodbusters, faced many hardships. One problem they had was the lack of trees for building cabins. They overcame this difficulty by digging blocks out of the thick prairie sod.

Definitions
1. A wide area of flat or gently rolling land with tall, coarse grass and few trees
2. A house built of blocks cut from the sod; sod flowers cover the house in the spring.
3. One hundred sixty free acres of land on which any person could settle if he improved the land

Write the definitions by the correct word.

Prairie

Homestead

Sod house

Sharpen Your Skills! Write the letters.

It

Use with Lesson 46

Nebraska's Tornado Watches

name _____

Tornadoes form into funnel shapes as they twist across the sky and swoop to the ground. Their powerful winds cause a thunderous roar, louder than a freight train. Tornadoes can cause damage by blowing down buildings or lifting cars into the sky. During tornado season the Weather Bureau watches for tornadoes and issues warnings, which have saved many lives.

Read each word. Write the sentence from the paragraph that describes the tornadoes' appearance, sound, and effect.

Appearance—

Sound—

Effect—

SHARPEN YOUR SKILLS! **Write the letters.**

U u

The Song of Kansas

name _____

Write the words of the song on handwriting paper.

Home on the Range
Oh, give me a home where
the buffalo roam,
Where the deer and the
antelope play;
Where seldom is heard a
discouraging word,
And the skies are not
cloudy all day.

Although we usually think of the whole western range when we hear this song, Kansas adopted it as its own in 1947.

SHARPEN YOUR SKILLS! Write the letters.

V v

Use with Lesson 48

Eisenhower's Home

name _____

Though he was the commander of the Allied Armies during World War II and later President of the United States, Dwight Eisenhower was proud of growing up in the town of Abilene, Kansas. He once said, "I come from the very heart of America."

"Soldiers, ... I have full confidence in your courage, devotion to duty and skill in battle. We will accept nothing less than victory."
General Eisenhower
on June 5, 1944

Write the words of General Eisenhower on the lines below.

SHARPEN YOUR SKILLS! **Write the letters.**

Ww

Use with Lesson 49

Minnesota Winter

Write the poem on handwriting paper.

The people of Minnesota bundle up for winter weather. The temperature usually ranges between 2° F and 15° F, but the record low temperature is -59° F.

Minnesota Skates

Minnesota winds will sting
As round the lake on silver wings
The whirling, twirling skate blades sing.

Minnesota skaters bold
Brave the snow and bitter cold
To race on ice as bright as gold.

Minnesota winters long
Seem to pass by like a song
While the skaters glide along.

Sharpen Your Skills!

Write the letters.

X x

Bread and Butter State

name _____

Minnesota, the "land of a thousand lakes," has fertile soil and clean rivers.

Alphabetize Minnesota's chief farming and fishing products.

Farming Products

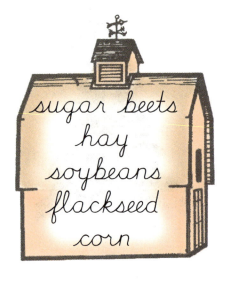

- sugar beets
- hay
- soybeans
- flackseed
- corn

Fishing Products

- catfish
- chubs
- tullibee
- buffalo fish
- yellow pike

Sharpen Your Skills!

Write the letters.

Yy

56

Use with Lesson 51

New World Symphony

name _____

The European composer Anton Dvořák, lived for a while in America. Visiting Iowa, he was inspired by the sights and sounds to write the New World Symphony. It is filled with the music of America. On the last page of the music, Dvořák wrote, "Thank God!" His music reminds us to be thankful for the blessings God has bestowed on our land.

Write a list of sights in America you think may have inspired Dvořák to write the New World Symphony.

_____
_____
_____
_____
_____
_____
_____
_____

SHARPEN YOUR SKILLS! **Write the letters.**

Use with Lesson 52

The Corn State

name _____

Prize Corn Bread

2 C. cornmeal ½ t. salt
1½ C. buttermilk ¼ t. soda
2 t. baking powder ¼ C. corn oil

Heat oven to 450°. Place greased skillet in oven to heat. Measure meal, baking powder, salt, and soda into mixing bowl. Add shortening and milk. Blend thoroughly. Pour batter into hot greased pan. Bake 15 minutes or until golden brown.

Iowa's nickname is the "Corn State." People also call it the "Land where the tall corn grows."

Write the recipe.

Gateway to the West

name _____

By the Mississippi river in St. Louis lies the Jefferson National Expansion Memorial Park. The great arch there has been nicknamed the "Gateway to the West."

- **It was built to honor Thomas Jefferson, the Louisiana Purchase, and the western pioneers.**
- **Capsule cars carry people to the top.**
- **The arch was finished in 1965.**
- **The arch is 630 feet high.**

Answer all the questions to make a paragraph.

1. Why was the arch in St. Louis built?
2. When was it completed?
3. How high is it, and how can you travel to the top?
4. What is its nickname, and why do you think it is called that?

_____
_____
_____
_____
_____
_____
_____
_____
_____

Missouri's Botanical Garden

name _____

Missouri Botanical Garden, St. Louis, photo by Jack Jenning

The famous Missouri Botanical Garden grows more than 12,000 species of plants and trees. But most people visit to see the beautiful flowers that fill the air with the scent of spring year-round.

Center the words of the song as you write them on handwriting paper. Decorate the wide borders as they might be seen in a poetry book.

Thy Word Is Like a Garden, Lord
Edwin Hodder

Thy Word is like a garden, Lord,
With flowers bright and fair;
And everyone who seeks may pluck
A lovely cluster there.

Thy Word is like a deep, deep mine,
And jewels rich and rare
Are hidden in its mighty depths
For every searcher there.

Ringling Brothers Circus

Five Wisconsin brothers had a talent for performing. Their small act grew into the huge Ringling Brothers Circus.

Write a poster to advertise the Ringling Brothers Circus.

SHARPEN YOUR SKILLS! Write the letters.

Use with Lesson 56

61

Laura Ingalls Wilder

g j y z

Laura Ingalls Wilder was born in the woods of Wisconsin. Her books tell the story of pioneer life.

Write each title correctly on the line below it.

little house in the big woods
_____

farmer boy
_____

little house on the prairie
_____

on the banks of plum creek
_____

by the shores of silver lake
_____

the long winter
_____

little town on the prairie
_____

these happy golden years
_____

the first four years
_____

The Great Chicago Fire

On October 8, 1871, Dwight L. Moody preached to a large crowd. He did not know that he would never see some of the people again. By the end of the service, the great Chicago fire had started. It burned more than one-third of the city to the ground. Because of the fire, God gave Moody a burden for souls.

Write the quotation on handwriting paper.

"I do not know anything America needs more today than men and women on fire with the fire of heaven: not great men, but true, honest persons, God can use."

— D. L. Moody

Sharpen Your Skills!

Write the letters.

f g

Use with Lesson 58

John Deere

name _____

The Illinois prairie sod stuck to the wooden plow blades as farmers tried to plow. Then John Deere invented the steel plow. It dug clean furrows and saved farmers hours of backbreaking labor.

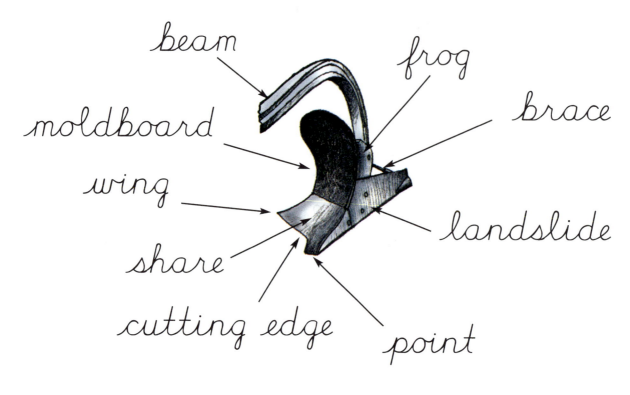

Write the parts of the plow in alphabetical order.

1. _____
2. _____
3. _____
4. _____
5. _____

6. _____
7. _____
8. _____
9. _____

Write the letters.

_p_ _____

64   Use with Lesson 59

State Flag Insert

The following pages contain flags for use on the introduction pages of each geographic region.

They are arranged according to the place they appear in the book.

The number by each state name is the order in which it entered the Union and officially received statehood.

Throughout the year you will match the number of each flag with the same number of the worktext page. Then you will write the state name on the line by the matching number.

California	Oregon	Washington	Alaska
31st State	33rd State	42nd State	49th State

Hawaii	Idaho	Nevada	Utah
50th State	43rd State	36th State	45th State

Colorado	Wyoming	Montana	Arizona
38th State	44th State	41st State	48th State

New Mexico	Oklahoma	Texas	North Dakota
47th State	46th State	28th State	39th State

South Dakota	Nebraska	Kansas	Minnesota
40th State	37th State	34th State	32nd State

Iowa	Missouri	Wisconsin	Illinois
29th State	24th State	30th State	21st State

Michigan	Indiana	Ohio	Arkansas
26th State	19th State	17th State	25th State

 Louisiana 18th State
 Mississippi 20th State
 Alabama 22nd State
 Tennessee 16th State

 Kentucky 15th State
 West Virginia 35th State
 Georgia 4th State
 Florida 27th State

 Virginia 10th State
 North Carolina 12th State
 South Carolina 8th State
 Maryland 7th State

 Delaware 1st State
 Pennsylvania 2nd State
 New Jersey 3rd State
 New York 11th State

 Connecticut 5th State
 Rhode Island 13th State
 Massachusetts 6th State
 Puerto Rico

 Vermont 14th State
 New Hampshire 9th State
 American Samoa
 U.S. Virgin Islands

 Maine 23th State
 Guam
 Northern Marianas

Tulip Festival

name _____

Every May Holland, Michigan, turns into a Dutch village, as the people host the annual Tulip Festival.

Write a title for each picture.

_____

_____

_____

_____

_____

_____

_____

_____

_____

_____

_____

_____

_____

_____

_____

_____

_____

_____

SHARPEN YOUR SKILLS!

Write the letters.

b f h k l

Use with Lesson 60

69

Paul Bunyan

name _____

Paul Bunyan, the legendary lumberjack, spread his camps across the North. Many stories about him began in the forests of Michigan.

Write a description of each character.

_____
_____
_____
_____
_____
_____
_____
_____
_____

Sharpen Your Skills! **Write the letters.**

𝒹 𝓉

Johnny Appleseed

name _____

It is said that the apple orchards of Indiana began as seeds from the pocket of Johnny Appleseed.

Use your own words to write the legend about Johnny Appleseed.

_____
_____
_____
_____
_____
_____
_____
_____
_____
_____
_____
_____
_____

Indiana's Poet

name _____

James Whitcomb Riley traveled across Indiana writing poetry that painted a picture of life in the Midwest.

Write the poem on handwriting paper.

"Old Bob White"
James Whitcomb Riley

Old Bob White's a funny bird!—
Funniest you ever heard!—
Hear him whistle, — "Old—Bob—White!"
You can hear him, clear from where
He's 'way 'crosst the wheat—field there,
Whistlin' like he didn't
care — "Old—Bob—White!"

Ohio's Soap Box Derby

name _____

Children from ages 11 to 15 have designed, built, and driven their own motorless race cars since the Soap Box Derby started in Ohio in 1934. The rule book states that each car must weigh less than 250 pounds with the driver in it. The nose of the car cannot be too sharply pointed, and every car must have a drag brake. After the race cars are inspected, the Soap Box Derby begins.

On the lines below write a list of Soap Box Derby rules from the information given.

_____
_____
_____
_____
_____
_____
_____
_____
_____

Compare your posture, paper position, and pencil hold to that of the boy on the inside back cover of this book.

Use with Lesson 64

Thomas Alva Edison

name _____

Thomas Edison always seemed to be asking questions as a boy in Milan, Ohio. Many of his questions could not be answered. Edison had to find out for himself. By the end of his life, he had invented hundreds of things, all because he wanted to know more.

On handwriting paper write the list of Edison's inventions in alphabetical order.

moving picture camera

carbon telephone transmitter

phonograph

dictating machine

battery

fluoroscope

Neatness counts!
Cross out mistakes.

Erase smudges.
Don't wrinkle paper.

Ink Pens

name _____

1. Hold your pen just as you would hold a pencil.
2. Line up your paper with writing arm.
3. Do not use a pen that blots or skips.

Use an ink pen as you write a description of an interesting site in your state.

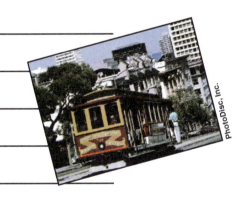

Use with Lesson 66

Southern States

Glue the flags in the correct places. Write the names of the states in the blanks.

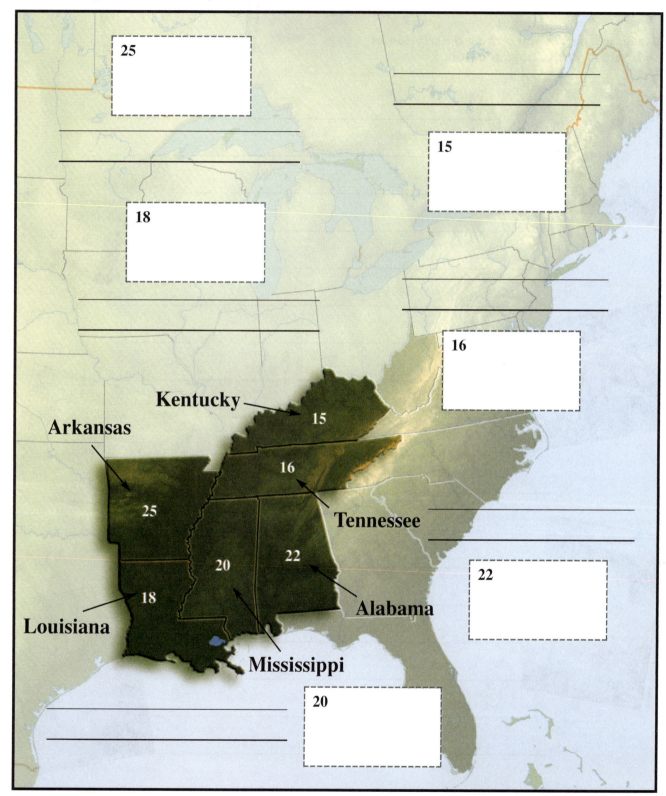

name _____

SOUTHERN STATES (CONT'D)

Glue the flags in the correct places. Write the names of the states in the blanks.

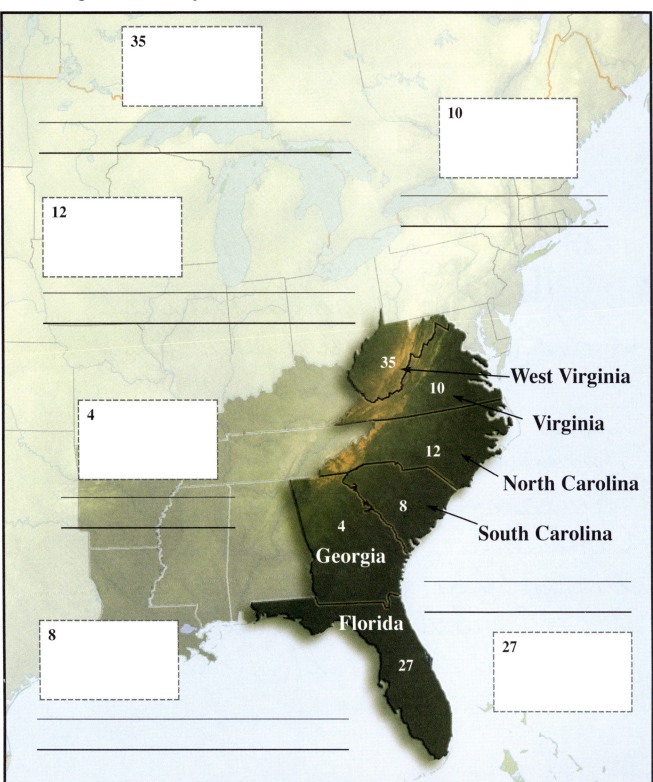

Use with Lesson 67

77

Civil War

Correct Mistakes. ~~Arkansaw~~ Arkansas

Write the paragraph on handwriting paper.

During the Civil War, Arkansas's neighbors fought each other with rifles and cannons. For several years Arkansas had two capitals—one Union and one Confederate. In 1865 the South surrendered. The War Between the States ended, as well as the war within the state of Arkansas.

Diamond Hunting

name _____

Write smoothly to avoid fat/thin and light/dark words

Shine Shine

Of all the states, only Arkansas has a diamond field.

Write the words of the hymn on handwriting paper.

When He Cometh
by Rev. W. O. Cushing

When He cometh, when He cometh
To make up His jewels,
All His jewels, precious jewels,
His loved and His own:

Like the stars of the
    morning,
His bright crown adorning,
They shall shine in their
    beauty,
Bright gems for His crown.

John James Audubon

name _____

When Louisiana was still wilderness, John James Audubon settled there to study and draw pictures of wild birds. He noted their habits, nests, eggs, and nestlings. His published work made him famous.

Fill in the bird observation report.

When did you last see a bird? _____

What color was it? _____

Where did you see it? _____

What was the bird doing? _____

Were other birds with it? _____

Have you seen other birds like it? _____

What kind of bird do you think it was? _____

Cajun Frenglish

Focus on joints. _Cajun_

In the 1700s the English drove out the Acadian people from their homes in Canada. Some of the Acadians settled in southern Louisiana. They became a distinct culture called Cajun. Even today Cajun culture influences the food, language, and music of Louisiana.

Write the Cajun words and their translations.

Maringouin—Mosquito   Bon—Good

Ouaouaron—Bullfrog   Oui—Yes

Tu parles Cajun?—Do you speak Cajun?

Mississippi Riverboat

name _____

Sweep out joints at the midline. *boat   river   whistle*

Complete the story.

Some day I want to be a riverboat pilot.

Use with Lesson 72

Pick a Bale of Cotton

name _____

Sweep out joints at the base line.   *bale   pick   summer*

Write the words of the song.

Years ago, cotton pickers often sang as they gathered the cotton from the fields. Nowadays cotton is picked by large machines.

Pick a Bale o' Cotton
Oh, jump down,
*   turn around,*
Pick a bale o' cotton.
Oh, jump
*   down, turn*
*   around,*
Pick a bale
*   a day.*

Use with Lesson 73

From Alabama

name _____

Many young men from Alabama followed the '49 Gold Rush to California. Their favorite song was "O Susanna."

O Susanna
Stephen Foster

I came from Alabama with my banjo on my knee.
I'm going to Louisiana my truelove for to see.
It rained all night the day I left, the weather
   it was dry.
The sun so hot I froze to death, Susanna don't
   you cry.

Write the words of the song below.

_____
_____
_____
_____
_____
_____
_____
_____
_____
_____

George Washington Carver

name _____

George Washington Carver urged the people of Alabama to plant peanuts since the boll weevil was destroying the cotton. But no one knew what to do with the peanuts after that first harvest. Carver experimented and found hundreds of uses for them.

shampoo, axle grease, soup, mayonnaise, coffee, peanut butter, ice cream, flour, bleach, linoleum

Write in alphabetical order the list of products made from peanuts.

1. _____
2. _____
3. _____
4. _____
5. _____
6. _____
7. _____
8. _____
9. _____
10. _____

Tennessee's Scopes Trial

Two-Stroke letters. F H K X Q

Write the name of the lawyer with the correct view. Then on handwriting paper, write the paragraph in your own words.

The Case
In Tennessee the law in 1925 stated that evolution could not be taught in public schools. Mr. Scopes, a science teacher, broke the law and was arrested.

Clarence Darrow
Evolutionist

Mr. Darrow called witnesses to testify that evolution was a scientific theory that students should believe. Evolutionists believe that man came from a one-celled animal that changed and improved until it became man. Clarence Darrow claimed that evolution could be taught from the Bible.

William Jennings Bryan
Fundamentalist

Mr. Bryan explained the Bible and Creation. He showed how the Bible taught that man had not evolved and become better, but had fallen because of sin. Finally, Mr. Bryan told the jury that evolution is not true and that sinful man needs to be saved through the blood of Christ.

Which lawyer was right?

The Verdict
Mr. Scopes was found guilty of breaking the law and fined $100.00.

Tennessee's Frontiersman

Two-Stroke letters. *t x*

Davy Crockett grew up on the wild frontier of Tennessee. Since few school teachers lived near Davy, he did not learn to read or write until he was an adult.

Later, Crockett ran for office as a U.S. Congressman to represent his wilderness state.

During his campaign, he often joked. Once a flock of guinea hens flew near the platform by his opponent. Their "Cr-cr-kt" sound disturbed the man, so Davy turned it into a joke.

On handwriting paper write the joke Davy Crockett told.

"I told him he had not had the politeness to name me in his speech, and that when my little friends the guinea fowls had begun to holler, 'Crockett, Crockett, Crockett,' he had been ungenerous enough to drive them all away."

Use with Lesson 77

The Bluegrass State

name _____

Write the words of the song on handwriting paper.

Dotted letters. *i j*

My Old Kentucky Home
Stephen Foster

Weep no more, my lady,
oh! weep no more today!
We will sing a song for the
old Kentucky Home,
For the old Kentucky home,
far away.

Kentucky Horses

name _____

Horses thrive on the rich bluegrass of Kentucky.

Write the name of each breed of horse.

Thoroughbred

_____

_____

Appaloosa

_____

_____

Morgan

_____

_____

Palomino

_____

_____

Quarter horse

_____

_____

Arabian

_____

_____

Use with Lesson 79

Brother Sheffey

wrong   **right**

Oval letter form.

Circuit-riding preachers had a big task in the rural southern communities of the early 1800s. There were not enough preachers for each tiny country church.

Robert Sheffey, one such preacher, walked and talked with the Lord. He carried a sheepskin in his saddle as he traveled his preaching circuit in West Virginia and nearby states. At any time of day or night Brother Sheffey would spread out his sheepskin and pray. He knew God heard and answered prayer.

Robert Sheffey served as preacher and pastor of hundreds of country people for half a century.

And whatsoever ye shall ask in my name, that will I do, that the Father may be glorified in the Son. If ye shall ask any thing in my name, I will do it.

John 14:13–14

Write the verses.

The Dulcimer

name _____

In the mountains of West Virginia, many folks build dulcimers to play during long winter evenings.

Always proofread to check for mistakes.

Describe the dulcimer. Then proofread the description.

Use with Lesson 81

91

The *Monitor* and the *Merrimack*

During the Civil War, Virginia witnessed the first battle between iron-clad ships, but neither of them won.

Finish the rhyming word beside each word below. Be sure it relates to the battle between the *Monitor* and the *Merrimack*.

rattle	battle
broke	s_____
chip	s_____
wiring	f_____
bells	s_____
suns	g_____
giver	r_____
pocket	r_____
wreck	d_____
lock	d_____
tailors	s_____
gravy	n_____
sort	p_____

Use with Lesson 82

Virginia's Shenandoah Valley

Poetry and songs use indented lines.

The beautiful Blue Ridge and Allegheny Mountains of Virginia form the Shenandoah Valley.

> Shenandoah
> Oh, Shenandoah, I long to hear you,
>   Away you rolling river
> Oh, Shenandoah, I long to hear you
>   Away, I'm bound away,
>   'Cross the wide Missouri.

Write the words of the song. Indent correctly.

Blackbeard in North Carolina

name _____

For a while Blackbeard left pirating and lived in North Carolina to abide by the King of England's proclamation.

Write the proclamation below.

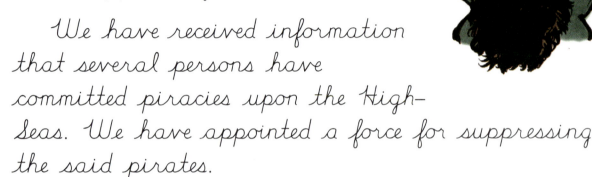

By the King
A Proclamation for
Suppressing Pirates

We have received information that several persons have committed piracies upon the High-Seas. We have appointed a force for suppressing the said pirates.
   The fifth day of September 1717
   King George

The First Gold Rush

name _____

In 1799 twelve-year-old Conrad Reed found a golden rock glinting in a sunlit stream near his North Carolina home. When he picked it up, it seemed to be heavier than lead. The town silversmith thought it was worthless because it wasn't silver. Conrad's father finally sold the 17-pound rock for $3.50. The jeweler who bought it discovered it was almost pure gold. The word spread like wildfire: "There's gold in them thar' hills!"

Rewrite the story as if you were Conrad Reed telling about your discovery of gold.

_____
_____
_____
_____
_____
_____
_____
_____
_____
_____
_____
_____

South Carolina's Zoo

name _____

Question Mark ?

The zoo in Columbia, South Carolina, is a world famous zoological park.

On handwriting paper, write several of the questions the class must have asked.

Dear Fourth Graders,

You asked many interesting questions in your letter. I hope I can answer all of them satisfactorily.

First, the reason we don't put animals in cages is that we want them to live as if the zoo were their home in the wild. Very few animals ever escape.

We don't allow visitors to feed the animals because animals don't eat that way in the wild.

The rainstorm you saw in the bird forest was created by a computer. We have these showers twice a day.

We keep mother animals and their babies in separate rooms so that humans won't bother them. The mothers take better care of their babies that way. I hope you were able to see some of the babies on the closed-circuit television.

I'm glad you enjoyed your trip to Riverbanks Zoo. I'm always happy to answer your questions.

Sincerely,

The Zookeeper

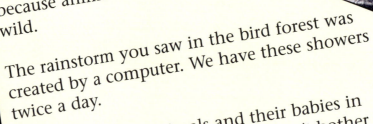

The Huguenots

The shores of America welcome the persecuted of other lands. The Huguenots found this welcome as they arrived in South Carolina.

Outline form: I.
　　　　　　　　A.
　　　　　　　　B.

Arrange the outline correctly as you write it below.

II. The French government persecuted the Huguenots.
　　B. John Calvin left the Catholic church.
　　A. John Calvin believed in God's Word.
 I. John Calvin led the Huguenots.
　　A. The Huguenots faced persecution bravely.
　　B. Many Huguenots escaped and fled to South Carolina.

　　　　　　　　The Huguenots
I. John

Joel Chandler Harris

name _____

Joel Chandler Harris heard many stories on the plantations near his boyhood home. Later he wrote them down for a newspaper and then for a book. All of his life he collected the Br'er Rabbit tales.

Write the sentences beside the correct picture.

- The clumsy, stupid, crotchety bear lived near Br'er Rabbit.
- The villain of the stories was the enemy of Br'er Rabbit.
- The defenseless hero trickster joked to escape tight spots.
- The small land tortoise knew almost as many tricks as Br'er Rabbit.

Br'er Rabbit

Br'er Rabbit

Br'er Fox

Br'er Fox

Br'er Tarrypin

Br'er Tarrypin

Br'er B'ar

Br'er B'ar

98

Use with Lesson 88

Stone Mountain of Georgia

name _____

Stone Mountain is the largest rock dome in North America. It covers a two mile area and rises 700 feet.

The mountain features a carved memorial to southern Confederate leaders. This carving shows Jefferson Davis, Robert E. Lee, and Stonewall Jackson on horseback. The sculpture is ninety feet high.

Unscramble the words to make sentences about Stone Mountain.

1. Stone Mountain a huge is mass of granite. light gray
2. is the It stone largest mountain in North America.
3. 1,683 is It feet sea level. above
4. displays mountain The carving a War Civil of heroes. huge

> Margins are imaginary lines on both sides of your paper.

_____
_____
_____
_____
_____
_____
_____
_____
_____

Florida Everglades

name _____

Indent correctly when using outline form.

Write descriptive phrases in the correct places on the outline.

I. Unusual plants of the Everglades
   A.
   B.

II. Strange animals of the swamp
   A.
   B.

Citrus Fruit

name _____

Citrus growing and processing is Florida's most famous industry. Oranges are the most important crop, but Florida also grows grapefruit, limes, and tangerines as well as many hybrids.

The first citrus tree seeds were thought to have been brought from Spain by Ponce de Leon in 1513. Today Florida is a leading producer of the nation's citrus products.

Neatness counts. Don't smudge ink.
Cross out mistakes. Write smoothly.

Write a brief description of your favorite citrus fruit. Discuss size, color, taste, and food value.

_____
_____
_____
_____
_____
_____
_____
_____
_____
_____
_____
_____
_____
_____
_____
_____

name _____

NORTHEAST STATES

Glue the flags in the correct places. Write the names of the states in the blanks.

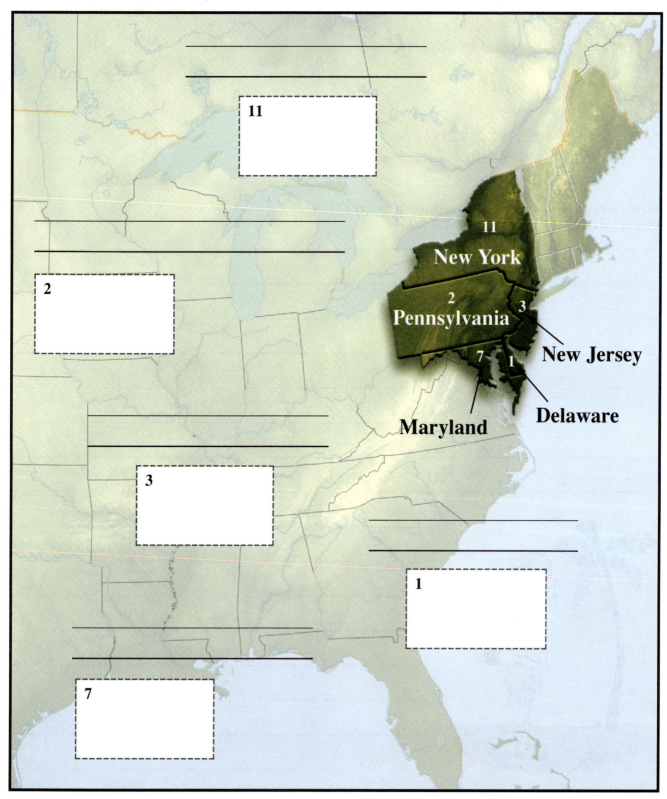

102 Use with Lesson 92

name _____

NORTHEAST STATES

Glue the flags in the correct places. Write the names of the states in the blanks.

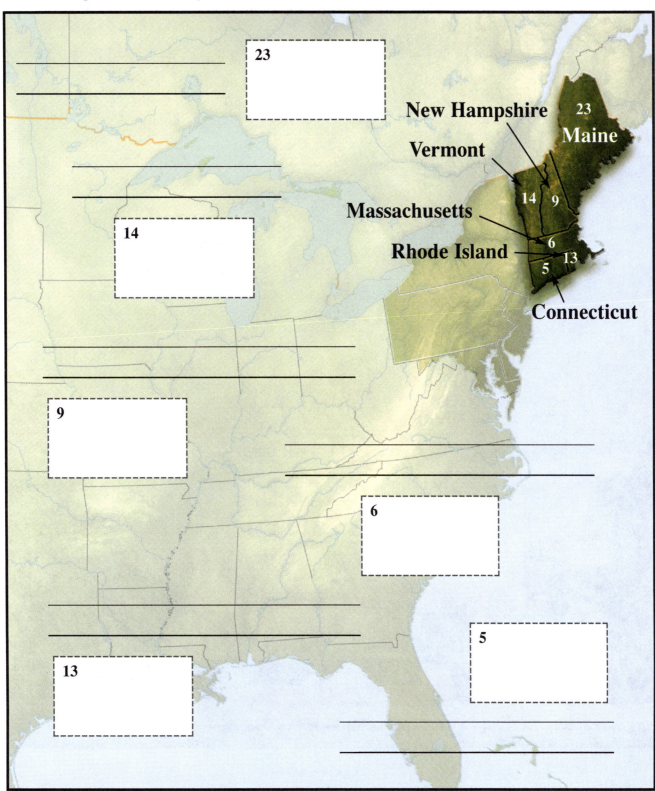

Use with Lesson 92

103

Washington, D.C.

name _____

Write the paragraphs on handwriting paper.

The small state of Maryland gave 69 square miles to the United States for the site of the nation's capital. President George Washington chose the land himself. In 1793 he laid the cornerstone for the Capitol building.

Over 50 years later the Capitol was completed. Then in 1863 the Statue of Freedom was lifted to the dome to represent freedom for America.

Morse Code

name _____

The first Morse code telegraph was sent from Washington, D.C., to Baltimore, Maryland.

A	B	C	D	E	F	G
•—	—•••	—•—•	—••	•	••—•	——•
H	I	J	K	L	M	N
••••	••	•———	—•—	•—••	——	—•
O	P	Q	R	S	T	U
———	•——•	——•—	•—•	•••	—	••—
V	W	X	Y	Z		
•••—	•——	—••—	—•——	——••		

Decode the first message sent by Morse code. Rewrite the message on the line below.

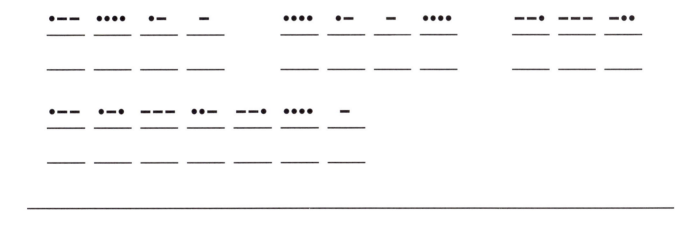

_____

Write a Morse code message. Decode it below.

_____

_____

Use with Lesson 94

105

Letter Size

name _____

Check Letter Size
Use a ruler to draw a midline.
Most lowercase letters should not reach above it.
Descenders should never go below it.

Write your favorite verse. Check the letter size. Rewrite any words containing wrong-sized letters.

Grandfathers

name _____

The Delaware Indians did not have an alphabet. They kept track of their history on the "Walam Olum." The "Walam Olum" is a piece of wood with stories painted on it. Other tribes did not keep track of their histories because they had no system of writing. These tribes respectfully called the Delaware Indians "Grandfathers."

Write a paragraph that tells about an event that is an important part of your family's history on handwriting paper.

Delaware

Write the paragraph on handwriting paper.

Delaware has several nicknames. It earned the name "The First State" in 1787 when it ratified the new U.S. Constitution before any other state did. Another nickname, "Blue Hen State," came from the War for American Independence. The Delaware soldiers battled like fighting cocks of a famous blue hen. Both nicknames remind the people of Delaware to be proud of their state.

Hans Brinker

Indent the beginning of every paragraph.

From her home in New Jersey, Mary Mapes Dodge wrote a book about life in Holland.

"Anyone may enter for the prize," Hilda said.

"Oh, jufvrouw, even if we could enter, we could skate only a few strokes with the rest. Our skates are hard wood, you see. They soon become damp, and then they stick and trip us," said Hans.

"I cannot buy you each a pair of skates, but here are eight kwartjes," Hilda smiled.

Write the paragraphs from the book *Hans Brinker*.

Baseball in New Jersey

name _____

Labels must be written clearly and placed correctly.

The first recorded baseball game took place in Hoboken, New Jersey, on June 19, 1846. The "New Yorkers" beat the New Jersey "Knickerbocker Club" 23 to 1.

Fill in the blanks with the correct labels.

Pitcher *First Baseman* *Left Fielder*
Shortstop *Second Baseman* *Center Fielder*
Batter *Third Baseman* *Right Fielder*
Catcher

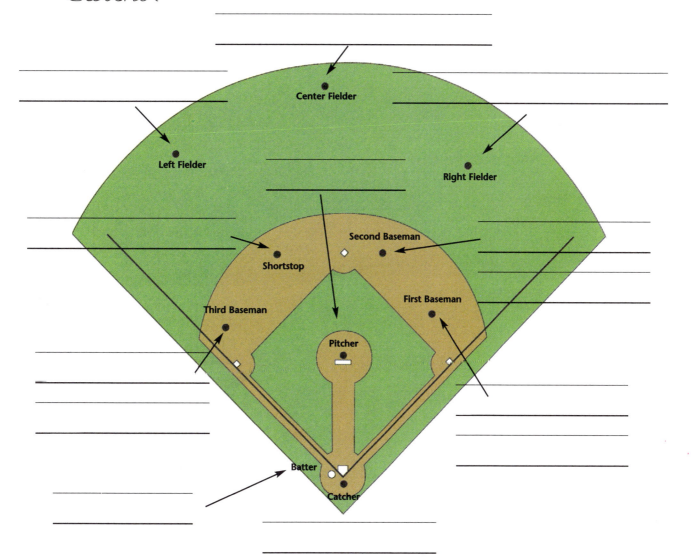

Use with Lesson 99

Gettysburg Address

Quotation marks
" "

President Lincoln dedicated the Civil War cemetery in Gettysburg, Pennsylvania, with these words.

Write the quotation on handwriting paper.

"Four score and seven years ago, our fathers brought forth on this continent, a new nation. . . . We are met on a great battlefield. We have come to dedicate a portion of that field. . . . That this nation, under God, shall have a new birth of freedom, and that government of the people, by the people, for the people, shall not perish from the earth."

Abraham Lincoln

Use with Lesson 100

Shoofly Pie

The Pennsylvania Dutch bake a mouth-watering molasses pie called Shoofly Pie.

Write the recipe on handwriting paper.

Mix until crumbly.
    1 C. flour
    ¼ C. butter
    ½ C. brown sugar

Dissolve and set aside.
    1 C. molasses
    1 C. hot water
    1 t. baking soda

Pour filling into unbaked pie crust.
Sprinkle the crumb mixture on top.
Bake 35 minutes at 375°.

Use with Lesson 101

New York's Metropolitan Opera

New York is the center of many cultural events. People travel from all over to see the museums, art galleries, and libraries. One of the most famous places is the Metropolitan Opera.

Here is an excerpt from the opera *William Tell*. The tyrant Gesslar tries to trap the hero William Tell.

In a play or drama, indent the spoken parts, but not the names.

Gesslar: Thou art by all accounted a bowman yet unequalled. Upon thy son's head place this apple. Thy arrow I would see with sure aim pierce it. If not, thou and he die.

Write the words from the opera.

_____
_____
_____
_____
_____
_____
_____
_____

Erie Canal

name _____

When a line of poetry or song does not fit on one line, divide the line and indent the second part.

The Erie Canal stretches across New York, joining the Great Lakes to the Atlantic Ocean.

Erie Canal
I've got a mule, her name is Sal,
Fifteen miles on the Erie Canal!
She's a good old worker and a
　　good old pal,
Fifteen miles on the Erie Canal!
We've hauled some barges in
　　our day,
Filled with lumber, coal and hay,
And we know every inch of the way,
From Albany to Buffalo.

Write the American folk song.

_____
_____
_____
_____
_____
_____
_____
_____
_____
_____

Use with Lesson 103

Skips and Jumps

I pledge allegiance to the flag of the United States of America and to the Republic for which it stands, one Nation under God, indivisible, with liberty and justice for all.

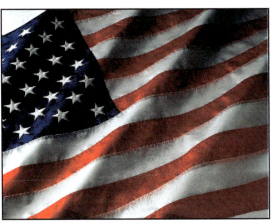

Cross and dot letters after writing the whole word.

Write the pledge to the American flag.

_____
_____
_____
_____
_____
_____
_____

Use with Lesson 104

Legibility

If your writing can be read, you have written legibly.

If letters or words in your writing are confused or misread, they are illegible.

How many reasons can you list for writing legibly? Write them below.

_____
_____
_____
_____
_____
_____
_____

Nathan Hale

name _____

After completing the page, fill in the self-evaluation.

	😊	🙂
Space between letters		
Space between words		
Space between lines		

Nathan Hale grew up in Connecticut. During the War for American Independence, he spied on the British. He was caught and sentenced to death. His last words inspired Americans to fight on for their freedom.

Write Nathan Hale's famous last words.

I only regret that I have but one life to lose for my country.

_____
_____
_____

Write your opinion telling why Nathan Hale was a hero.

_____
_____
_____
_____
_____
_____
_____
_____
_____
_____
_____
_____

Webster's Dictionary

name _____

After completing the page, fill in the self-evaluation.

	😀	😊
Slant of lowercase		
Slant of uppercase		
Consistent Appearance		

Noah Webster of West Hartford, Connecticut, wrote spellers, readers, and grammar books. Then he started on his most famous book, Webster's Dictionary. When completed, it contained 70,000 words and helped to standardize the English language.

Use your dictionary to find a definition of each word. Write each on the lines.

dictionary—

definition—

word—

Use with Lesson 107

115

Rhode Island Castles

name _____

The castles and mansions of Rhode Island are filled with wonderful sights.

After completing the page, fill in the self-evaluation.

Slant of lowercase		
Slant of uppercase		

On handwriting paper, write a description of the Rhode Island castle.

_____
_____
_____
_____
_____
_____
_____
_____
_____
_____
_____

116

Use with Lesson 108

Cliff Walk

name _____

The Case
The estate owners raised iron fences around the cliffs to keep the fishermen off their land.

The fishermen demanded a pathway around the shoreline of their island.

The Verdict
The estate owners could not block the fishermen's path.

Conclusion
The estate owners built a beautiful pathway among the cliffs. The fishermen and the estate owners enjoyed the path.

Write the court case below.

_____
_____
_____
_____
_____
_____
_____
_____
_____
_____

Massachusetts' Cranberry Bog

name _____

Cranberries grow on the sandy coast of Massachusetts. Indians called these berries *sassamanesh.* They taught the pilgrims to pick the tart red berries and cook them.

When the berries ripen in September, the harvesters scoop them up. Before long the cranberries find their way into pies and puddings, juice and relish. Best of all, cranberries always find their way into Thanksgiving Day feasts.

Write as many words as possible, using the letters in the title.

Massachusetts Cranberry Bogs

Use with Lesson 110

Jonathan Edwards

name _____

1 2 3 4 5 6 7 8 9 0

Jonathan Edwards carefully observed the world around him. From the time he first learned to talk, he questioned everything he saw. The Bible told him that God created the earth, and Jonathan believed the Bible, but he did not have Christ as his personal Savior. Finally, at the age of seventeen, Jonathan accepted Christ. He became one of the greatest preachers in America.

Luke 13:19 *Job 36:27*
Job 37:9 *Ecclesiastes 11:7*
Job 22:12 *Psalm 77:18*

Write the correct Bible reference beside the observation of nature mentioned.

Effect of sunlight _____

Growth of trees _____

Substance of fog _____

Cause of lightning _____

Direction of the wind _____

Nature of the stars _____

Use with Lesson 111

Smuggler's Notch, Vermont

name _____

Cc Aa Oo Qq Gg Ee

Smuggler's Notch is a thin pass between Mount Mansfield and the Sterling Mountains. During the War of 1812, smugglers hid food and other goods brought from Canada in the caves of the pass. The cold underground air kept the food from spoiling. As time passed, the pass was nicknamed "Smuggler's Notch."

Complete the smuggler's journal entry.

Tonight we will reach the notch. The food will be left in a cave.

Use with Lesson 112

Vermont's Maple Sugar

name _____

Maple sugar is made every spring in the towns and villages of Vermont.

Write the steps for sugaring off.

Tap a maple tree; add a spout.

Catch the sap in a bucket.

Collect the sap every day.

Boil the sap in an open kettle.

Wait for the sap to thicken.

Pour the syrup on hot johnnycakes.

New Hampshire's Astronaut

Ll Bb Hh Kk Nn Mm Pp Rr

Alan B. Shepard of East Derry, New Hampshire flew into space May 5, 1961.

Read the answers Alan B. Shepard might have given. Guess what the questions must have been and write them above the answers.

Reporters:

Shepard: Yes, I was the first American in space.

Reporters:

Shepard: I flew in the *Freedom 7* Space Capsule.

Reporters:

Shepard: It lasted fifteen minutes from launch to splashdown.

Reporters:

Shepard: I circled one hundred sixteen miles above the earth.

Reporters:

Shepard: NASA awarded me the Distinguished Flying Cross.

New Hampshire's Mt. Washington

name _____

Vv Xx Ww Uu Yy Zz

- An 8-mile road leads to the summit.
- In 1934 the speed of the wind was measured at 231 miles per hour.
- A small steam train uses a ton of coal and 1,000 gallons of water to travel to the top.
- The peak of Mount Washington reaches 6,288 feet into the sky.
- No trees grow above 4,800 feet.

Write a paragraph using the information.

Use with Lesson 115

Stormalong

name _____

> Stormalong, or Stormy, as his shipmates nicknamed him, sailed the seven seas. His gigantic ship, built from the tall, straight pines of Maine, dug the Panama Canal trying to reach the Pacific Ocean.
>
> No port in all of Maine could hold that ship or Stormy. He may have grown up on the coast of Maine, but salt got into his lungs, and he felt at home only on the wide, wide ocean.

Write a paragraph telling of Stormalong's adventure.

_____
_____
_____
_____
_____
_____
_____
_____
_____
_____
_____

Maine's Country Fair

name _____

As summer ends, the towns in Maine often hold Country Fairs. Games keep the children busy, while the adults earn prizes in contests. And everyone enjoys the delicious foods.

Write the foods or events under the correct headings.

pie-baking contest

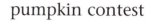
pumpkin contest

greased pig

FOOD
_____
_____
_____

pig-raising contest

weiner roast

CONTESTS
_____
_____
_____

three-legged race

pie-eating contest

GAMES
_____
_____
_____

clam bake

egg toss

candied apple

cotton candy

wheelbarrow race

Use with Lesson 117

Map of the United States of America

Which letters do you need more practice writing?

_____
_____
_____
_____
_____
_____
_____
_____
_____

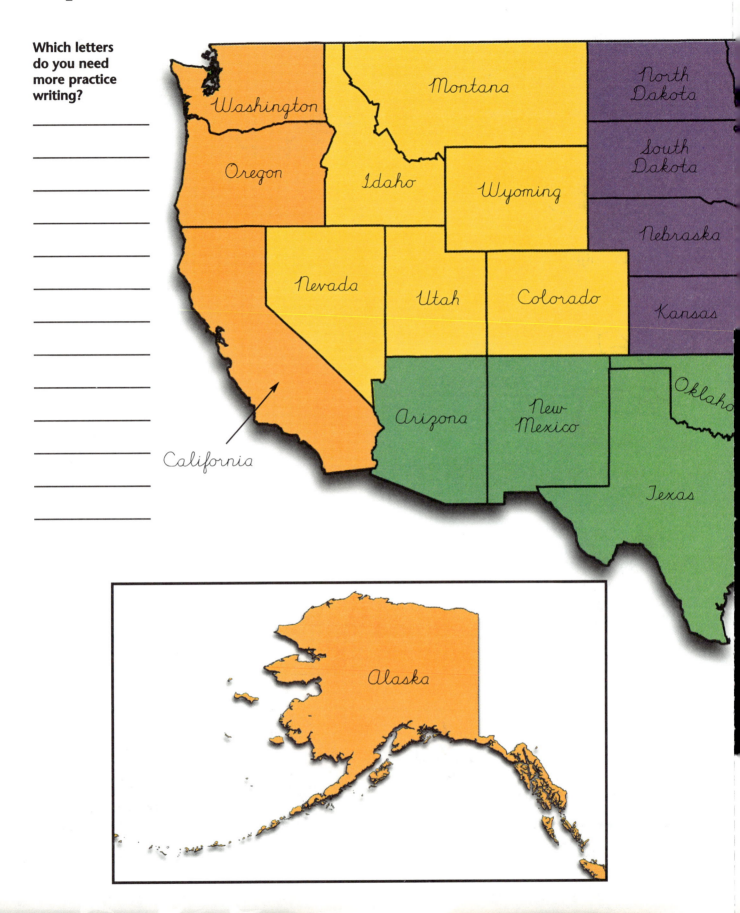

Which letters are easiest for you to write?

America

Write the words of the hymn "America, the Beautiful."

"Blessed is the nation whose God is the Lord: and the people whom he hath chosen for his own inheritance." Psalm 33:12